GRACIE'S garden

LARA CASEY
ILLUSTRATIONS BY JON DAVIS

B&H kids
Nashville TN

To my little gardeners.
I love you from my head tomatoes.

Copyright © 2020 by Lara Casey
All rights reserved.
978-1-0877-0626-9
Published by B&H Publishing Group, Nashville, Tennessee
Hand lettering by Valerie McKeehan
Dewey Decimal Classification: C635
Subject Heading: GARDENING/PATIENCE/MIRACLES
Printed in Dongguan, Guangdong, China, March 2020
1 2 3 4 5 6 • 24 23 22 21 20

Gracie and her sweet sister Sarah and her crunchy munchy brother Joshua really liked dirt. Especially the dirt in Gracie's garden! It was full of flowers and friends and sometimes buried treasure!

Dirt was fun.
Dirt made cities.
Dirt made tea parties.
Dirt made Mom chase them with the hose!
And dirt made things grow.
Things like tomatoes and
cucumbers and corn.

Gracie's Garden

Bee Happy

Come in for
Peas and Quiet

FREE WEEDS!

Joshua ate veggies right out of the garden. He loved to snack on them— especially the tomatoes!

Joshua snacked on them so much that one day they were all gone. He made an official request to the gardener, Gracie, for more tomatoes of all kinds.

Red ones. Green ones. Purple ones. Striped ones. Bumpy ones. Big ones. Itty-bitty ones.

Gracie ran into the house and came
back out with a tiny envelope.
"Ta-da!" said Gracie.
Her tomato-loving brother was confused.
"Those must be some *tiny* tomatoes in there!"

Gracie opened the envelope and took out a little dot. "This teeny tiny speck is a *seed*!" she explained.

"But how is that little thing going to turn into tomatoes for me to eat?" asked Joshua.

"God puts little miracles inside each seed!" said Gracie. "Do you know what a miracle is, Josh? It's when something so wonderful happens that you can't explain it because it's so amazing!"

"Like pizza!" said Joshua.

Gracie giggled. "People can make pizza. Only God can make seeds," she said. "He grows a little miracle inside each one for us to see!"

"But I can't seeee it," said Sarah.

"If we share some peaches with Nutty the squirrel, he'll tell us more," said Gracie. "He knows all about things that grow because he eats most of them!"

Nutty was nuts about peaches and happy to help his three garden buddies. "Well, mister crunchy munchy Joshua," said the furry friend, "pull up a pumpkin and sit down on your bumpkin."

Joshua chose a pumpkin and sat on his bumpkin. Gracie sat down on the candytuft plants in her rainbow pants. And Sarah just sat down.

"Wet me tell woo (*munch, munch, munch*) about the magic in a seed," Nutty said with full cheeks. "You see, inside a seed God puts everything it needs! He can grow big things from the tiniest seeds.

"Acorns grow into huge oak trees to have picnics under . . . unless I eat the acorns first. And peach seeds grow into trees that make yummy scrumptious peaches."

"Unless you eat them first!"
said Gracie with a laugh.

"Do you know where your carrots come from?" asked Nutty. "A seed so tiny you can barely see it! God gave each seed a secret code that tells it how to grow and what to turn into. It just knows!

"A tomato seed knows to grow into a tomato, not a potato. A squash seed knows to grow into a squash, not a Josh.

"And a watermelon seed knows to grow into a watermelon, not a—

18

tomato

potato

squash

Josh

FLUFFY KITTY!"

19

"Growing things is simple! First you dig a hole in the dirt," said Gracie the gardener. "Then put the seed in the hole. Add a little water. Some sunshine. And voila! You wait for the magic to happen!"

"But I can't seeee it!" said Sarah.

"You can't see it yet, but little by little, it's happening," said Gracie. "Just wait. We have to be patient. It means to wait and see."

"So how many minutes till I can eat tomatoes?" asked Joshua.

Gracie did some thinking. "About 115,200 for this kind of tomato. Eighty days."

"Eighty days?!" said Joshua. "That's like one hundred years! I'll have twinkles by then!"

"I think you mean wrinkles," said Gracie. "But you won't have twinkles or wrinkles. You'll have tomatoes! God grows flowers and trees and squirrels and brothers and sisters and all good things little by little by little by little.

"And we can do *lots* of fun things while we wait on the seeds to sprout and make tomatoes for you to eat!"

"We can paddle.

We can battle.

We can saddle.

We can skedaddle."

"Or we can . . .
wheeeee!!!" said Sarah.

"I could climb trees," said Joshua. "Or build with sticks. Or make my famous mud soup!"

"You sure could," said Gracie.

And so they did. Gracie and her sweet sister Sarah and her crunchy munchy brother Joshua crafted and played and made lots of mud soup!

Joshua tried new garden recipes. Gracie jumped rope.

Sarah picked flowers for Mom.

They watched their little seed sprout
and grow and bloom. They tried to keep
Nutty away from the peaches . . . and
Fluffy Kitty away from Nutty!

And before they knew it . . .
eighty or so days later . . .

Green Zebra
Tomato

Early Girl
Tomato

Sungold
Tomato

Cherokee
Purple
Tomato

Mr. Stripey
Tomato

Chocolate
Stripes
Tomato

"TOMATO! TOMATO! TOMATOOOO!" said Sarah.

"It's a mirror call!" Joshua said with excitement.
"You mean a miracle!" said Gracie.
"I can see it!" Sarah said with joy.

"Miracles are yummy!" said Joshua.
Little by little, that tiny seed had
turned into the happiest tomato dance
you ever did see!